Guy Fawkes

The Gunpowder Plot of 1605

By
Andrew Thompson

"Remember, remember!
The fifth of November,
The Gunpowder treason
and plot;
There is no reason
Why the Gunpowder
treason
Should ever be forgot"

Guy Fawkes Day is celebrated every year on the 5th of November.
It is also sometimes called 'Gunpowder Plot Day'.
This is the story of Guy Fawkes and what happened to make the
5th of November become so famous in English history.

It all started when a few Catholic men, over-zealous for their religion, decided to destroy King James I of England, as well as the Houses of Lords and Commons also known as Parliament. Their plan was to use gunpowder to blow up the Houses of Parliament, kill the king and replace him with a Catholic king.

It was all the plan of one man named Robert Catesby, but he was quickly joined in his murderous plot by several other conspirators. The most famous of these men was

Guy Fawkes.

Guy Fawkes was tall and strong. He was an Englishman, born in York, who had fought bravely with the Spanish army in Flanders and was considered just the man for the job. So he was brought over to England to carry out the plot, and with the other plotters, he took a vow of secrecy.

The plot was simple.

They rented a house near to the building where the Parliament met. The plan was to dig an underground passageway between the two buildings, and then to plant gunpowder under Parliament House. However, they quickly had some problems in carrying out their deadly scheme. Firstly, the walls where they had to dig the underground passageway were too thick.

They abandoned this plan, and instead, they rented a cellar right under the House of Lords. This would make it far easier. They put thirty-six barrels of gunpowder into this cellar, and so in May 1605, all was ready to blow the King and his Parliament up into the air!

But wait! Parliament did not meet until the 5th of November!
And by that time the secret plot had been leaked.
Some believe that a mysterious letter was sent by one of the plotters,
Francis Tresham, to his brother-in-law Lord Monteagle, warning him
of the coming disaster and the cellars under Parliament House.
Immediately the cellars were searched, and the gunpowder was
discovered along with Guy Fawkes who was hiding nearby guarding
the explosives and waiting for the right time to set them off.

Whether true or not, in any case, that was the
end of the gunpowder plot!

Guy Fawkes was arrested early in the morning of the 5th of November by a Westminster magistrate and a party of soldiers. He was locked up in the Tower of London where he was tortured over the next few days and confessed to wanting to blow up Parliament.

When the other plotters heard that the plot had failed they quickly fled to the country. But they were too late. Most of the men were captured, and eight were tried for high treason along with Guy Fawkes.

All were found guilty and sentenced to the worst punishment, which was to be hanged as traitors in St. Paul's Churchyard, in Westminster, London. But immediately before his execution on 31 January, Fawkes fell from the scaffold and broke his neck.
He was 35 years old when he died.

The Parliament announced a national day of thanksgiving to celebrate it's survival, and set for the day the attack would have taken place, the 5th of November. The first celebration was held on the 5th of November, 1606.

Today, all these hundreds of years after this gunpowder plot was discovered the 5th of November - Guy Fawkes Day - is still remembered as a national holiday, and is celebrated with feasts, and the lighting of large bonfires and fireworks. Straw men designed to look like Guy Fawkes called 'Guys' are often burned as well.

While this story started in England, the tradition of the 5th of November celebration later spread to other places around the world, including Canada, South Africa, and Australia.
This event is also known as Bonfire Night.

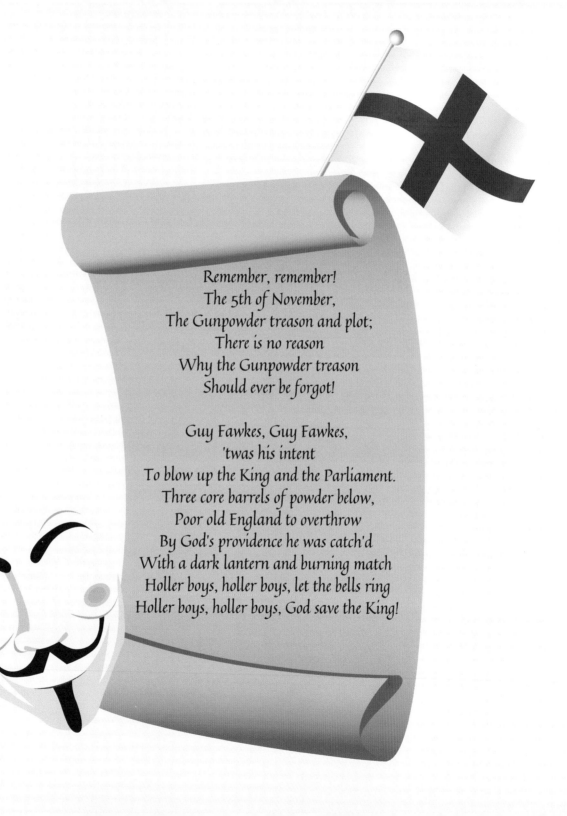

Remember, remember!
The 5th of November,
The Gunpowder treason and plot;
There is no reason
Why the Gunpowder treason
Should ever be forgot!

Guy Fawkes, Guy Fawkes,
'twas his intent
To blow up the King and the Parliament.
Three core barrels of powder below,
Poor old England to overthrow
By God's providence he was catch'd
With a dark lantern and burning match
Holler boys, holler boys, let the bells ring
Holler boys, holler boys, God save the King!

Guy Fawkes and his co-conspirators

Clothing at the time of James I

Pikemen at the time of James I

Typical Style duing the reign of James I

Vintage image of the Tower of London at the time of James I

Printed in Great Britain
by Amazon

28870687R00016